Saint Patrick
An Ancient Saint for Modern Times

Edmond Grace SJ

First published in 2019 by Messenger Publications

The material in this publication is protected by copyright law. Except
as may be permitted by law, no part of the material may be reproduced
(including by storage in a retrieval system) or transmitted in any form or
by any means, adapted, rented or lent without the written permission of
the copyright owners. Applications for permissions should be addressed
to the publisher.

The right of Edmond Grace SJ to be identified as the
author of the Work has been asserted by him in accordance with the
Copyright and Related Rights Act, 2000.

ISBN: 978 1 78812 0197

Copyright © Edmond Grace SJ, 2019

Designed by Messenger Publications Design Department
Typeset in Times New Roman and Masqualero Regular
Printed by Nicholson & Bass Ltd

Messenger Publications,
37 Lower Leeson Street, Dublin 2
www.messenger.ie

ABBREVIATED TITLES

The Confessions of Saint Patrick (CP)
Letter to the soldiers of Coroticus *(LC)*

CONTENTS

CHAPTER 1

One Day on Fifth Avenue

St Patrick, darling and patron saint of Ireland, is a friendly face in the month of March when winter can seem to linger, uninvited. People love to see him coming through the streets on 17 March with his staff, green poncho and pointy bishop's mitre hat. Patrick has always been popular and this is no accident: he knows how a good story can enhance a profile. Down the years he has reinvented himself with regularity and ingenuity.

Everyone knows about St Patrick and the snakes, even if some insist that there were never any snakes in Ireland. If the snake story was pure invention, it was a very successful invention. It is a delightful and charming story, charming enough to ensure that the legend of Patrick and the snakes will never go away. Patrick was good and the snakes were evil, and he banished evil from Ireland. He protected us all.

'Patrick the shape-shifter' was a well-known story in ages past. It is said that one day, in order to escape his enemies, Patrick turned himself and his eight companions into a small herd of deer. There is no doubt that he eluded his enemies many times if not always in the form of a deer. Even if 'Patrick the shape-shifter' is a bit exaggerated, it is good a story that won people's attention in a world where there were no newspaper headlines, no nine o'clock news and no smart phones. We might describe the incident as fake news – 'BISHOP TURNS HIMSELF INTO STAG' – but those who spread this news did so with a single-minded conviction that we can only admire. They wanted everyone to know and love Patrick.

'Patrick and the shamrock' is another wonderful story that tells us how he explained the faith to ordinary people. Have you ever smuggled a magnifying glass into our national museum in Kildare Street? Have you ever held it up before the Ardagh or Derrynaflane chalice and gazed at the intricate detail of these astonishing works of art? Have you ever stood before one of the great Irish high crosses and examined it closely? None of these ancient items carry so much as a single shamrock. That would all come much later, at a time when the Catholics of Ireland were denied the joy of open worship.

They would come together in some muddy and remote place and, keeping their heads down for fear of the authorities, would 'get' Mass. One day someone was looking down at the ground as usual and they saw a small three-leafed plant. They must have stooped down and plucked that little plant and waved it at the priest who said, 'That's the very same three-leafed shamrock that Patrick used to talk about the Blessed Trinity!'

The story of St Patrick and the shamrock must have spread like wildfire. The shamrock will never be put back in its box.

Patrick is about to reinvent himself again in a story that has never been told before. I saw it happen with my own eyes.

Having been living in New York for almost a year I stopped one day at Saint Patrick's Cathedral on Fifth Avenue, inside I found a woman deep in prayer with a true and transparent devotion. Even decades later I can sense her presence. There was no doubt in my mind that she was praying to St Patrick. I could see her looking at his statue high up in a niche with his nineteenth-century bishop's outfit – crosier, mitre, vestments and beard.

What was my reaction? I was not moved, as I should have been by so obvious a show of devotion, instead I was intrigued. The woman was African-American, and I wondered why she might be praying to St Patrick, the patron saint of Ireland. The answer came to me after I stepped outside. She was praying to a man who had been taken by force across the sea and condemned to a life of slavery. He would escape from slavery – and from that land – but he returned to live among the people who had enslaved him, enduring much at their hands but living with a faith that enabled him to triumph over hardship.

For me, she changed the story of St Patrick. She loved him as much as I did and could relate to him in a way I never could. Thanks to her, the story of Patrick can never be put back in its little Irish box.

Did you know that Patrick wrote the first two books to come out of Ireland? One is called *The Confession*, which is quite short, and then there is 'the letter to Coroticus' which is even shorter. You might say that they are too short to be called books but they were the first of their kind and, in those far off days, they had no competition. There would not have been a single bookshop in sight.

Patrick tells us that he spent his first sixteen years in a place called Bannavan Taberniae in 'Britannia' that might have been Britain but might also have been Brittany. There are those who debate these matters with much learning and vigour, but I myself have no great appetite for taking sides on these matters. My preference is for indisputable facts or, failing that, the entertainment value of a good story.

Take, for instance, the story of Croagh Patrick. After having prayed for forty days and forty nights on the holy mountain Patrick faced down the devil – like a sheriff in a cowboy film – and, as a result, all the snakes of Ireland had to pack their bags and leave. I love that story about the snakes and I love that mountain. I first climbed it with my father when I was twelve years old on Reek Sunday in 1965 with thousands of others. (Twenty seven years later I would climb it carrying his ashes). Down through the centuries thousands and thousands and thousands have climbed the Reek. They might even have climbed in pagan times to worship some god whom Patrick would later push aside. That mountain has been made holy by all those feet and the prayers that came with them – even the prayers of pagans. Let no one tell you that the story of Patrick on the Reek is untrue unless, of course, you want to confine yourself to facts.

One fact is beyond dispute: Patrick's land is Ireland and I am proud to be one of his fellow Irishman, even if he did say that the place was 'at the ends of the earth'. He was a holy man but he was not perfect and if he was less than complimentary about Ireland we must remember that, in those days, nobody knew what lay beyond the Atlantic. If Patrick knew about California he probably would not have spent so long in Ireland!

His ignorance of the other side of the Atlantic means that Patrick is now patron saint of Ireland but, prompted by that good woman in New York, I am putting him forward for an additional job – patron saint of the reconciliation of peoples.

CHAPTER 2

The Story of Patrick's Big Brother

On one particular morning in north-western Europe, at a time when the world was falling apart, a sixteen year old lad was waking from sleep. He loved the empire though he might not have been thinking of it at that moment. As a child he would have heard his father, Calpurnius the deacon, and his grandfather, Potitus the priest, speaking of the great Christian empire of Rome. As long as he could remember he had known about the glory of it all, even in these difficult times, and he was not to know – not yet – that this glory was disappearing like the sun beneath the horizon. Unlike the sun the glorious empire of Rome would never rise again, but it endured in the imagination of a boy who would later insist that his Irish Christians should be treated as Roman citizens.

He expected his fellow citizens to respect the law and he would have heard from his father that the baptised must never be reduced to slavery. They would not, for one moment, have been thinking of the Irish who were wild savages. Calpurnius and Conchessa, his wife, hated the Irish. As they stood there on that day watching the Irish sailing away with their boy, they cursed those barbarian pirates.

Patrick would return to his family and his relatives after he escaped from Ireland, but we don't know how many brothers and sisters he had or where he came in the family. He might have been the oldest but maybe he had a big brother and perhaps, if you dig into a ditch near Bannaven Taberniae, you might well find the traces of some sodden parchment that once carried these words:

> Empire? I see no empire! It might have been there for some people at some time in the past but where was it when the Irish came to take my little brother? Did anyone order the legions to go and find him and slaughter his abductors and bring him back home? And what about the thousands like him who were taken off into slavery? We were convinced he was lost to us and possibly dead when suddenly he reappeared. We could not believe our eyes, but it was clear from the start that the Irish had done something to him. He was saying prayers all the time and he kept talking about God. When he told us that he had had a vision of the people of Ireland calling him back it was too much for us. We didn't want to hear about it and then he left us a second time and never returned. The Irish took my brother away from us, not once, but twice and that worthless half-dead empire of Rome allowed it to happen.

We don't know if Patrick had a big brother, but we do know that when Patrick exported those first two books from Ireland they were written in Latin, which means they were not written for the Irish. Patrick wrote about himself as living 'among barbarian people, a stranger and exile for the love of God'. He talked of wanting to visit his family and 'the Christian community in Gaul' but he tells us that the Spirit would mark him out as guilty if he left Ireland and that 'I am afraid of wasting the labour which I have begun'. If he could not go home he would write and it was clear that he wanted to explain himself to the people back home, whom he had left long ago and who would never see him again: 'Although I am imperfect in many ways I want my family and my relatives to know what kind of man I am so that they can understand the desire of my soul' (CP, 6).

In spite all those years preaching the Gospel in Ireland, he would never stop thinking about where he came from. No matter how highly he was thought of and no matter how much he loved the Irish and their music, this place was not where he came from. It was not the place of his childhood. It was not where he lived during his time as a student. Patrick was lonely for his own people. He missed them, even at the end.

CHAPTER 3

Roman, and Proud of it

Patrick was proud to belong to an empire with a great past but it had little or no future and you might accuse his father, Calpurnius, and his grandfather, Potitus, of not preparing the young man for the harsh future that lay ahead. They might have been well advised to get him to face the truth with plain words, 'forget about all that Roman Empire stuff. It's time has come and gone'.

In those days the glory of the Roman Empire was like a building slowly crumbling into ruin. Not much happens from day to day, until, one morning, everyone can see that a floor has collapsed or a wall has caved in.

When Patrick woke up on that day when his life was turned upside down, he was from a family of some standing. He might have been looking forward to traveling the world for a few years in his early years of adulthood. He almost certainly found the place a bit dull – until those Irish pirates arrived. Later, as he tended sheep on some cold hillside, he must have thought that he came from a place called heaven. Perhaps it was just as well that he grew up with notions of grandeur. Maybe they helped the young slave to hold his head high and to tell people that his name was Patricius which meant 'patrician'. His people were no mean people.

There was that moment when he was fourteen, maybe fifteen when, within the space of half an hour, he did something that would later cause him shame. He does not say what happened though he did tell a friend about it years later. Whatever he did caused him much grief and serious self-doubt.

For many years he was able to bury the episode down inside himself. He might have forgotten all about it, because he tells us that in those early teenage years he and his friends paid little attention to what they heard in church.

His carefree life was about to change, however. That woman in New York would identify with what happened the day Patrick was seized by Irish pirates. Her ancestors found themselves in the hold of a ship as they were carried across the Atlantic – a much longer journey. The journeys were different but destination was the same – slavery.

Thomas Jefferson, third president of the United States, owned slaves and one of them, James Hemings, trained as a top class chef. Jefferson later gave Hemings his freedom and offered him a paid job doing what he used to do as a slave, but Hemings decided to get employment elsewhere. When Jefferson became president he was eager to have Hemings as his chef at the White House and Hemings really wanted the job, but there was a problem. In fact there were two problems. They both wanted the same thing but Jefferson could not bring himself to offer it and Hemings could not bring himself to ask for it. Both were paralyzed and it ended in grief when Hemings took his own life.

A similar story is told about Patrick and his owner, a man

called Miliuc. We are told that, when Patrick returned to Ireland, he went to meet this man and offered him the price of his own freedom. Miliuc could not bring himself to meet his former slave, so went into his house and shut the door and burnt the place down with himself inside it. Perhaps he was ashamed of what he had done to Patrick or perhaps he could not bring himself to come face to face with a man he had once owned in the way that you and I might own a cow or a dog.

There is something about slavery that cannot be painted in a picture. Nothing can capture what happens deep inside to those subjected to slavery and to those who participate in it.

On that first day when Miliuc sent him out onto the hillside to herd sheep, Patrick was sixteen years old, no longer a boy. He came from a proud family with high expectations of life and now he was a slave. For the woman in New York this story was part of her story. She understood it. But on that day in Saint Patrick's Cathedral I could only look on, not even recognising what I saw.

CHAPTER 4

Trouble and Prayer

People turn to prayer when they are in trouble. That woman who was praying to St Patrick in New York looked as if she once had troubles and was now deeply grateful; her ancestors, when they first came to America, certainly had troubles and like her they certainly did pray. They did what Patrick did and who would deny that people all over the world are still doing it? There are those who might be inclined to doubt the usefulness of this sort of thing but those prayers from people in trouble just keep coming.

   If you have an exam or eczema, an addiction, depression or cancer or if you have lost a friend the chances are that you will pray to God like those slaves in America and like Patrick himself. African slaves in America discovered Christianity, leaving behind the gods of their different tribes. Patrick also discovered Christianity because, even if he knew all about it before he came to Ireland, he did not know it as something real. Now he turned to God. He would rise to pray before dawn 'in snow and ice and rain'. In one day he would pray up to one hundred times and the same during the night: 'I never felt the worse for it, and I never felt lazy – as I realise now, the spirit was burning in me at that time' (CP, 16).

Prayer does something to you, especially when nothing is going right and you pray and pray. I have no doubt that St Patrick's New York friend knew this. I could tell, as she knelt there looking up at his statue, that something was on her mind – something that mattered deeply. She knew that Patrick would understand.

When you pray like that you let yourself be taken in. We tend to think of fools being 'taken in', being too easily deceived and shown up for the fools they are. The woman in Saint Patrick's Cathedral was clearly taken in but not as a fool. There was a peace about her – a sense of relief – like someone who is taken in out of the rain and the wind and given shelter. I have no doubt, as I watched her that day, that she had been given shelter. She had placed herself in God's hands and St Patrick had been of help to her. She could see him placing himself in God's hands out on that hill as the rain continued to fall and the wind continued to blow and the sheep continued to be stupid and Miliuc continued to be cruel. Patrick had found shelter and he was deeply grateful. Miliuc probably noticed that Patrick was grateful but not to him, and it would have made his anger burn. Miliuc could have had Patrick slaughtered like a sheep at any moment but he didn't and Patrick was grateful to his God, not to his owner.

Were the prayers of those early American slaves answered? We know that they began to read the Bible and the Bible gave them hope. Maybe Patrick had a Bible. Patrick might have remembered bits of the Bible, but it's unlikely that he would have remembered much, given how little attention he paid when he was in church as a teenager. That would not have stopped him praying as fervently as anyone. Do you have any difficulty thinking of those early Americans slaves crying out to God? We know that, when they read the Bible, they came across some words in the Book of Exodus:

> I have seen the misery of my people in this land. I have heard their cry. I know their pain. I have come down to deliver them from the land of the Egyptians and to lead them out of this land and into a good and broad land, into a land of milk and honey. (Ex 3:7–10)

We know that those words were read out loud and repeated many times and the voices that carried those words were heard by the people and the people raised their voices in reply. They prayed. How they prayed! They sang. How they sang! We sing those songs right here in Ireland to this very day.

Patrick never heard those songs, but perhaps he did remember that story from Exodus about when the Lord saw the misery of his people in a foreign land but, if he raised his voice, no one would have heard him except the sheep – and Miliuc. Imagine having to hear your own slave singing God's praise, even if he was a bad singer! It must have grated on Miliuc's nerves and perhaps he even had Patrick lashed for it.

Imagine if Patrick had become a time traveler and had made his way to eighteenth-century Virginia and found himself among the slaves of Thomas Jefferson. Patrick would have felt at home with James Hemings and his fellow slaves, except that Patrick's white skin would have left them confused. Imagine him arriving two centuries later at that cathedral on Fifth Avenue named after himself and watching that New York woman praying to that statue of a man in a nineteenth century bishop's outfit – mitre, crosier, vestments and beard.

Patrick prayed. No one can deny that, but did he pray for freedom? He does not say so. He just tells us that he prayed to God.

How did God answer his prayers?

CHAPTER 5

'In the Strength of God'

Patrick tells us that he heard a voice. It was a voice in the night, but not just in the night. Patrick heard that voice in his sleep: 'You have fasted well. Very soon you will return to your native country' (CP, 17).

He knew what that word 'fasting' meant. He was young and hungry for freedom. He had been in Ireland for six years and maybe God saw his misery just as he saw the misery of the Israelites in Egypt. Patrick tells us that God protected and consoled him 'as a father does for his son'. If you are having a good time you don't need protection or consolation.

Patrick tells us of another voice on another night: 'Look – your ship is ready' (CP, 17).

He knew the time had come to escape. It would turn out to be a journey of two hundred miles and he knew Miliuc would be coming after him. He might not have had those long eared bloodhounds used by American slave owners, but he must have had dogs sniffing their way through the countryside. For Patrick it must have been a hard and fearful journey.

There are many instances in ancient times of slaves being able to save up money and buy their freedom. There are even examples of people like Thomas Jefferson and Cicero setting slaves free without charging them for it but when a slave runs away it is an outrage. In Miliuc's eyes not only was Patrick a slave and a foreigner, he was a thief, stealing his own master's property.

Patrick tells us that he travelled 'in the strength of God who guided my way to the good' (CP, 17). He talks about 'my way', but how did he make his way? Was it by foot? Was it on the back of a stolen donkey? Who can tell? But the strength of God ensured that Miliuc never caught up with Patrick.

Some people must have given Patrick food because it would have been impossible to make that two hundred mile journey on an empty stomach. On the other hand he might have had to steal food. It is not a sin to steal food if you are starving.

We Irish were well known for our hospitality, even before the tourists arrived, and people have always welcomed travelers into their homes. This would surely have happened to Patrick and, after a good night's sleep, they might have given him bacon and eggs – with no fried tomatoes because tomatoes had yet to arrive from America. They would not have charged because in those days no one had a bed and breakfast business as we know it. Besides Patrick would have been too scrawny and they would have known that he had no money.

It must have been such a relief, when he finally made it to that ship. He must have wondered at times if God really had spoken to him and if that ship really was waiting at the end of the journey but his prayer was answered. The ship was real. That was the good news but there was also bad news because the captain took an instant dislike to him,

'Don't you dare try to come with us!'

We have said that Patrick did not have a particularly good singing voice and it is well known that people of poor singing talent are not good at adopting the accent of those among whom they live. If Patrick failed get a passage on a ship, sooner or later people would have noticed something strange about him. They would have looked at him with frowning faces and suspicious eyes: 'You are a foreigner from Britannia and you can't sing. You are also a Roman citizen and no Roman citizen, in his right mind, comes to this God-forsaken country unless he has been brought here as a slave! Who's your owner?'

As Patrick made his way back to his lodgings he began to pray and, even before he was finished, he was called back by the men in the ship: 'Come – we'll trust you. Prove you're our friend in any way you wish' (CP, 18).

In those days pagans expected to have their nipples kissed. This was their way of shaking hands but Patrick tells us that he refused to engage in this practice (CP, 18). He was hoping that they would come to faith in Jesus Christ and, with this in mind, he prayed to God as the ship set sail.

He was finally leaving Ireland. He must have been so happy. He must have given praise and thanks to God.

CHAPTER 6

A Journey with Dogs

Given the likelihood that dogs were used to sniff Patrick out after his escape, he might have been nervous in the presence of the ship's barking cargo, who might not have liked being bundled into a confined space. On the other hand they might have been friendly and Patrick might have earned his passage by feeding them during the three day crossing from Ireland to wherever they landed in the country of the Gauls.

As the craft sailed over calm waters and Patrick filled his lungs with sea air, perhaps he thought it all too good to be true. If so, he was right, because they landed in what he himself called a wilderness. They ended up wandering around for twenty-eight days and there was no sign of humanity anywhere. There might have been a war or a plague or a famine; it was as if the whole world was abandoned. Their food ran out and you might wonder why they did not decide to eat the dogs or why the dogs did not turn vicious and eat them. The captain turned to Patrick with a sneer on his face, 'Well, Christian? You tell us that your God is great and all-powerful. Why can't you pray for us, since we're in a bad way with hunger?' (CP, 19).

Patrick had probably been annoying them all with his prayers and his talk about God. The captain might have been hoping that Patrick's prayers would go unanswered and then they they would have an excuse to feed him to the dogs, but Patrick raised his voice and annoyed him even more: 'Turn in faith with all your hearts to the Lord my God, because nothing is impossible for him, so that he may put food in your way – even enough to make you fully satisfied! He has an abundance everywhere' (CP, 19).

Then something amazing happened, at least according to Patrick, who may be prone to exaggeration. Suddenly a herd of pigs appeared before their very eyes! They were not deceiving themselves. These pigs were real and they were able to prove this by slaughtering them and then cooking their flesh and, finally, eating it. They also fed some pig meat to the dogs who, like everyone else, were slowly dying of starvation.

They spent two nights in the place where they met the pigs. They gave thanks to God and treated Patrick with great honour, but that did not last. When they found some delicious wild honey one of them said that it must have been sacrificed to a god. Now it was Patrick's turn to be annoyed and, in protest at this blasphemy, he would eat none of it, which meant that the rest of them had that little bit more. At times his judgement was wanting.

The night after he refused the honey, something happened to Patrick which he would look back at with horror for the rest of his life. It was as if an enormous rock landed on him and he lost all the power of his limbs. Both then and in later years he believed that Satan was testing him. He cried out, 'Helias' but nobody is quite sure what that word means. Some say it refers to the words of Jesus on the cross: *'Eloi, Eloi lama sabachthani!'* or 'My God, my God, why have you forsaken me?' It might refer to the sun – '*helios*' in Greek. Later in his writings he would speak of Christ as the sun. Some people say 'Helias' refers to Elijah (CP, 20).

Patrick hardly knew anything about the Bible at that time, but he would soon learn a great deal and, by the time he came to tell the world about himself in his Confession, he placed bits of the Bible everywhere. By that stage he would have known about Elijah wandering through the desert on the run from his enemies and hiding in a cave on God's holy mountain. We are told that there was an earthquake, but God was not in the earthquake; there was a fire but God was not in the fire; there was a mighty wind but God was not in the wind. Finally, there was the sound of a gentle breeze and Elijah knew. He covered his face and came out of the cave to meet God.

Maybe something like that was happening to Patrick when he cried out *'Helias'*. Elijah must have been very frightened in that confined cave with the earthquake and the fire and the wind roaring outside. If God was not in the earthquake or the fire or the hurricane, then Elijah must have wondered if God had abandoned him. This might explain why Patrick would have called Elijah's name. There was a fear in Patrick, a terror, as that rock crushed down on him. Satan was testing him. He must have thought that the end had come and that God had abandoned him. Whatever he meant by that word *'Helias'* he wanted help – not any kind of help, but the kind of help that keeps Satan at a distance.

You may be wondering what happened to the dogs. We can be sure that they were thoroughbreds because no one would bother to transport mongrels across the sea. Most likely they were Irish Wolfhounds, which are enormous but, in spite of their size, are delicate and prone to sea sickness. Whatever happened to these particular dogs who travelled with St Patrick is lost to history, but their descendants are still around.

CHAPTER 7

'You'll Never Guess ...'

Patrick was now a free man. He was even freer than he was when he was sixteen in Banavan Taburniae. He was able to decide what he wanted to do without having to obey a slave master or even his parents. He was twenty-two when, at his own choice, he became a student in a monastery. Unlike when he was a slave on the mountains, he was not alone. Others were studying with him and, if the truth be told, most of them were better than he was at the study. He prayed frequently and, even if he was not as fired up as he was on the hillside, every time he prayed, he never regretted doing it. He was also learning a lot about the Bible. He made good friends with some, but only some, of the other students and later he would talk lovingly about 'the brothers in Gaul'.

Finally, after a few years, he decided to visit his family. It was the best part of ten years since that day when the slave traders came to take him. You might wonder what took him so long. You might well wonder, but no explanation is given.

Imagine his mother, Conchessa. She was still alive at this time because Patrick talks about visiting 'my parents'. They were both still alive.

His brothers and sisters, if they existed, would have welcomed him with open arms even if only for the sake of appearance. His turning up after all those years would have taken them by surprise. There would have been a magnificent feast with a fatted calf, pigs' heads, garlic and wine. Patrick probably did not have much to say because he might have been embarrassed by the fact that the family owned slaves. Having been a slave himself he knew what it was like.

That night Patrick had a dream. A man called Victoricus came and he was carrying a countless number of letters. He gave one of them to Patrick, who read what was written at the top of the page – 'The voice of the Irish'. As he read, he heard the people of the wood of Voclut 'near the western sea'. They were crying out with one voice, 'We beg you, holy boy; come and walk among us once again' (CP, 23).

This touched his heart deeply and he woke up.

Anyone, who knows anything about Patrick, knows about this dream and you would wonder what that woman in New York made of it. When her ancestors finally escaped from slavery they did not go back to Africa and they did not have dreams about the white people of the United States calling them back to walk once more among them. Yet, the late Martin Luther King was speaking with the voice of his people when he said, 'I have a dream that one day this nation will rise up and live out the true meaning of its creed that the sons of former slaves and the sons of former slave owners will be able to sit down together at the table of brotherhood'.

It would take many years for Patrick to see his dream fulfilled though he did tell his parents about it the next morning. He might have said, 'You will never guess what I dreamt last night'.

Whatever he said and however he said it, they were not pleased. They begged him, after all he had endured, to stay with them and not go away again but he turned their offer down.

Patrick left home for a second time, but this time it was of his own free will. There were no slave traders grabbing hold of him and he was no longer a teenager. He was turning his back on his family and answering the call of those Irish barbarians who had caused them all so much grief. Perhaps Patrick himself felt hurt and misunderstood and even angry with his family. His dream had brought him great joy. He might have heard, in the far distance, the music of the Irish but his family had seen it all as a kind of betrayal. Perhaps he was pleased to go.

Life is strange and none of us are perfect.

CHAPTER 8

What Patrick Learnt and Taught

Patrick spent a number of years as a student, probably at the bottom of the class. Having missed out on study in his teenage years and his early twenties Patrick, at the age of twenty-two, was finally beginning to catch up on his neglected education. It is no wonder that he felt inferior!

Some of his fellow students, who were well groomed and well connected, described him as *'rusticissimus'* which means (depending on your inclinations) bogman, yokel, bumpkin, slack-jaw or peasant. At times they might have called him 'sheep farmer' and, in his presence, they would complain about the smell. At other times they would call him the prodigal son and asked, with sneering tone of voice, when he planned to go back to live among the pigs. There must have been times when he would have preferred the lash of Miliuc's whip to the tongues of his new persecutors. Though we do know that he made at least one close friend (CP, 27–32).

You might well wonder whether he learned anything during those years, given his situation. The good news is that he did have something positive to show for his efforts, even if he never measured up to the standards of others.

The woman in New York might have been curious to know about Patrick's education and how he came to have an entire cathedral dedicated to him. Perhaps she went into the cathedral book shop and asked to buy a copy of *The Confession of Saint Patrick*. I imagine she would take it eagerly and open it up and, after reading a few paragraphs, she would have found this:

> There is no other God, nor will there ever be, nor was there ever, except God the Father. He is the one who was not begotten, the one without a beginning, the one from whom all beginnings come, the one who holds all things in being – this is our teaching. And his son, Jesus Christ, whom we testify has always been, since before the beginning of this age, with the Father in a spiritual way. He was begotten in an indescribable way before every beginning. Everything we can see, and everything beyond our sight, was made through him. He became a human being; and, having overcome death, was welcomed to the heavens by the Father. (CP, 4)

She would know that the way that the Son was begotten by the Father was indeed 'indescribable' and she would be thankful to St Patrick for reminding her.

> The Father gave him all power over every being, both heavenly and earthly and beneath the earth. Let every tongue confess that Jesus Christ, in whom we believe and whom we await to come back to us in the near future, is Lord and God. He is judge of the living and of the dead; he rewards every person according to their deeds. (CP, 4)

Her tongue would have confessed, like Patrick, that Jesus

Christ was Lord and God. It was not just her tongue. It was everything about her on that day when she knelt there looking up at the statue of St Patrick. You cannot pray to a saint in that manner unless you believe what the saint believes – that Jesus is Lord and God.

> He has generously poured on us the Holy Spirit, the gift and promise of immortality, who makes believers and those who listen to be children of God and co-heirs with Christ. This is the one we acknowledge and adore – one God in a trinity of the sacred name. (CP, 4)

Every time she went in and out of Saint Patrick's Cathedral on Fifth Avenue she blessed herself with holy water in the sacred name of the one God, Father, Son and Spirit. If Patrick was watching her, as I am sure he is, he would have been pleased. She was his friend and he would have stood at the elbow of the Son of God Himself, who pours out the Holy Spirit. He would have whispered in his ear: 'Don't forget my New York friend'. The Son of God would give him a disdainful look, because he never forgets anyone, but Patrick would take no notice of that, because he is determined to help his friend.

All this is very far removed from people studying for a university degree or a similar achievement. Of course, there is little point in studying anything, including the Bible, unless it affects your life or, better still, both your life and the lives of others. This explains why teaching is such a satisfying and rewarding activity.

Patrick's learning, such as it was, had a considerable effect on the Irish who lived at the ends of the earth. They listened. Some of them learned and some of them even became priests and bishops like him and so it has been ever since from generation to generation – in spite of wars, plagues, famines, persecutions and betrayals – to this very day.

CHAPTER 9

To the Rank of Bishop

When exam time comes around, students start behaving in a manner that would remind you of the hyena. They start sniffing all over the place for scraps of information, which they then keep to themselves. They have been known to tear pages and even entire chapters out of books to make sure that their fellow students never get to read them. In Patrick's day, before the electrification of student accommodation, they would steal candles from each other, not only to facilitate their own night time study but to prevent others from having light during those midnight hours when the student brain is at its best.

Patrick was happy enough when exam time came around, because the groomed-and-connected brigade started persecuting each other and they left him alone. Somehow he managed to get through – term by term, year by year. You might say he slipped through. Some may have fallen by the wayside but the rest finally reached the point where they were to be ordained as deacons.

Patrick was one of them but not before he had a last minute crisis. The memory of what he did at the age of fourteen was troubling him and he was beginning to wonder if he was worthy to be ordained. He knew he had to tell someone so he confided in a well-trusted friend, who was kind to Patrick. We are not told what happened next, but it seems that the ordinations went ahead as expected with Patrick as one of them.

The groomed-and-connected brigade all went for the plum jobs in the cathedrals of big cities where they hoped to get themselves noticed with a view to being made a bishop. The not so well connected members of the class went on to be ordained as priests. In those days priesthood was a dead end job and those with careers to think of remained on as deacons until the really big job came along. Priests were sent off to work in far-away parishes, where they would spend the rest of their lives. Most of them did not mind. They were happy to be looking after the people of God.

Patrick was probably sent to a far-away parish, at least for a while, but there were stirrings and soon something happened which made the groomed-and-connected brigade sick in the stomach. Everybody knew about Patrick and his dream. He would talk about the Irish calling him back to live among them and it made people laugh. They did not know that there were some good wise men among those brothers in Gaul. They listened to Patrick and his dream and they did not laugh.

News began to circulate that Patrick might be sent to preach the Gospel among the Irish, though some sincere people were opposed. They wanted to know why he would place himself in danger among a hostile people who did not know God. They did not have their way. Patrick was raised 'to the rank of bishop' (CP, 32).

That was really bad news as far as Patrick's persecutors

were concerned. They always had the highest opinion of the good wise men, which was only sensible, seeing that those men had much influence. Now those same wise men had honored Patrick's dream as a sign from God. He would return to Ireland, where he had spent six years as a slave, and he would now be marked by these words of Jesus himself:

> You have heard that it was said, 'You shall love your neighbour and hate your enemy'. But I say to you, love your enemies and pray for those who persecute you, so that you may be children of your Father in heaven; for he makes his sun rise on the evil and on the good, and sends rain on the upright and the wicked alike. (Mt 5:43–46)

The groomed-and-connected brigade could not endure the sight of the 'sheep farmer' being made a bishop, but they had to be there when it happened, pretending to pray for the new bishop with unconvincing stony faces. They had to queue up and ask for his blessing and they pretended to sing his praise, which they found both distasteful and exhausting. At the end of the day, they gathered round. They drank lots of wine and made sly jokes and sniggered.

Returning to Ireland was the first step in Patrick's long journey. A people at the edge of the world had carried him off to their land as a slave, like Joseph in Egypt, and now he would return to bring them the good news of Christ. The woman in New York understood what he had done because she knew her own people and their story. Patrick's journey will end when he becomes patron not just of Ireland but of the reconciliation of peoples.

When Patrick finally set out for Ireland, the groomed-and-connected brigade waved him off with much relief and they smiled humbly as they spoke to the old men, 'We always knew deep down that he would bring the gospel to the ends of the earth'.

They did not mean a word of it but saying things like that was good for their careers.

Patrick was returning to Ireland. When his New York friend thought about that moment of departure from Gaul she could see very clearly the reason why Patrick returned to bring good news to the Irish. He did it out of love. That dream about 'voice of the Irish' had awakened in him a love for the people of Ireland but that love did not come out of nowhere. It was God's answer to all those prayers he said on the hillside.

When he came home to his parents' house, he noticed the horses and the slaves and he remembered the slaves of his own family who had been taken away like himself by the Irish pirates. This memory had broken into the world in which he had grown up and to which he now had returned, if only for a brief visit. Through that breach, that very night, came that dream about the Irish but behind the dream there was someone who had never set foot anywhere near Ireland or, indeed, anywhere at all (CP, 23).

It was the Holy Spirit who made sure that the Irish wrote those letters in Patrick's dream. The Irish could not write in any language, never mind in Latin, so the fact that those letters came before the eyes of Patrick was nothing less than a miracle. The Holy Spirit rounded up those people near the wood of Vocult, wherever it is, and got them to call out. The Holy Spirit, because of Patrick's prayers, had placed in his heart that love for the Irish which has made Patrick famous today.

Patrick never really came to love the groomed-and-connected brigade with whom he studied – not in the way he loved the Irish – but those snooty brothers in Gaul were only small time persecutors, as we will see.

CHAPTER 10

The Ends of the Earth

The earth is round. We've known that for quite some time. You do not fall off the edge and you can travel wherever you like provided you have the technology. It was not like this in Patrick's day. He genuinely thought that he was at the ends of the earth and, of course, if you stand on the cliffs of Moher or on Dún Aongus or Slieve League or visit the deserted beaches of Connemara or Belmullet you will come away with the clear impression that they are at the edge of something beautiful and majestic. No edge is comfortable.

Patrick arrived at the edge of the world and the people who lived there were wild. There were lots of tribes fighting wars against each other, though war is probably the wrong word because it never lasted for more than a week of pillaging and, most of the time, it spread neither far nor wide. The trouble was that you never knew when or where a war would break out and who would be fighting against what enemy. Patrick needed protection – fighting men, preferably well connected sons of chieftains, who knew how to draw a sword and use it. The sons of chieftains got the best training in the use of arms and some of them knew how to handle diplomatically awkward situations.

Patrick would travel the country announcing the Good News and perhaps his bodyguard stood on each side of him, legs apart and swords at the ready. Perhaps they kept discreetly out of sight, but they were paid to be ready to come to his defence as Patrick raised his arms to heaven and called on his listeners to repent and believe the Gospel.

Many people in Ireland came to believe and they were baptised in the frost-bitten rivers of that rain drenched land. It seems that thousands were won over to the Lord and that many 'sons of the Irish and daughters of kings' became monks and nuns (CP, 41). He singled out one, only one, who must have made a big impression. She was 'of noble birth and very beautiful, already grown to womanhood' (CP, 42). She asked for baptism and, only a few days later, she said that a messenger of God had spoken to her asking her to become a virgin of Christ and 'in this way to draw closer to God'.

You might wonder what the relatives of these women thought of all this. They were not just unhappy. They were enraged and they made those women suffer for daring to reject both the gods of their ancestors and the scowling men who lusted after them. According to Patrick, those in slavery suffered most, 'They endure torture and constant threats' (CP, 42).

Patrick too had his troubles. On more than one occasion the young men, whom he had paid to protect himself and his companions, turned on them and robbed everything they had (CP, 52). He tells us of twelve attempts on his life and of how he was frequently taken captive – on one occasion for sixty days. He talks of many other conspiracies of which he was the intended victim and he himself had problems with lust, but he does not seem to have given in:

> The hostile flesh is forever dragging me towards death, that it, towards the satisfaction of unlawful desires, because I did not lead a life as perfect as other believers, but I confess it to the Lord and I do no blush in his sight because I am not telling lies. (CP, 44)

By the time Patrick wrote his *Confession*, there were thousands of Irish people baptised and building themselves into a Christian Church. Patrick wrote with great enthusiasm, as we have seen, of monks and nuns everywhere. You might wonder why he got so excited about monks and nuns who did not get married like most people. Of course, the monks and nuns spent time in silence and they chanted God's praise. People came to them and talked about their problems and asked them to pray, which you might not consider particularly useful, but those who asked for prayers were grateful. There was something else. Monasteries and convents, in those days, were places of peace, where no one carried spears or swords or hatchets.

Jesus of Nazareth, the Son of the eternal Father, laid down his life and conquered death. If he called on others to lay down their lives, it was nothing that he hadn't done himself and, if he asked men and women to live without wives or husbands, they were genuinely happy to do so even if they had problems with lust. Maybe, to distract themselves from those unlawful desires, they made themselves useful – caring for the sick, feeding the poor and teaching the young.

One side effect of all this activity was the emergence of a new industry. People would come from all over Europe to sit at the feet of Irish scholars. Irish monasteries, like Irish pubs today, were springing up all over Europe. They produced illuminated manuscripts by the thousand and these became the country's premier export along with monks, big dogs and butter. Music did not travel quite so well in the days before electronic recording.

Even further away into the future were the hospitals, schools, orphanages and churches built by the Irish all over the world, including Saint Patrick's Cathedral on Fifth Avenue where I saw that New York woman kneeling in prayer. We know that, when Patrick first started all this, it began to spread and the spreading continued without anyone suffering any of those unpleasant things which we associate with martyrdom. Given the fame of Irish for fighting, this absence of bloodshed at the introduction of Christianity is remarkable.

The people of Ireland took to Christ as if they were all waiting for a bus. The bus, driven by Patrick himself, would stop to collect passengers wherever it went and, as more and more people climbed on board, the bus got bigger and bigger. It travelled the length and breadth of the country with the passengers singing the praises of God at the tops of their voices. As for Patrick, he praised God and made an announcement to his passengers, 'I was like a stone sunk in the mud, but I was lifted up and placed on top of the wall!'

CHAPTER 11

Money Problems

Money is always a problem. We may have problems with health from time to time but most of the time we get over it. Money is different, we never have enough money – never – and the small, statistically insignificant number who are happy with what they have are singularly fortunate. Patrick was not one of those people. It is true that when he was a slave he would have got enough food and shelter to keep him alive and, in the fervour of his new found faith, he would have been content with anything but, once he returned to Ireland as a bishop, his money problems never ended.

We have already mentioned the bodyguards made up of sons of chieftains, who were accustomed to an expensive lifestyle. There were also women – you might call them ladies – who would place their ornaments on the altar as a contribution to Patrick's expenses. We will look at one particular incident that will help us understand how Patrick eventually got himself into trouble.

On one particular occasion a woman placed an expensive

piece of Celtic jewellery on the altar and Patrick refused to accept it. She insisted, reminding him that it was only right for her to support her bishop and, given that she was a woman of standing in the community, she was obliged to give a good example. Patrick listened with great courtesy but he was also adamant that she should take her jewellery and leave. Eventually she did so, feeling aggrieved and belittled by this foreigner who had rejected her generosity.

What made matters worse was that she suspected that he thought her motives were impure. That made her doubly angry, but she said nothing. She might have walked away with a pout on her face but, being a lady, she held her head at a discreetly measured angle.

Patrick hurt a considerable number of women in this manner but none of them said anything. He did not, in fact, doubt their motives but he did fear that, if he accepted any money from the newly converted Christians of Ireland, the work of God would be compromised. He would be accused of running a racket. He had baptised thousands and ordained many priests and, if he wanted to, he could have made a fortune, but he did it all for free. He also gave gifts to chieftains, above and beyond what he paid their sons, to keep them happy. When he wrote to the people back home he told them that he had spent upwards of the price of fifteen human beings on these items (CP, 53).

The people back home knew very well that he was spending a lot of money. Did he not get it all from them? Letters would arrive telling them of his exploits, which would have been as exciting as any television series, and they would always end with a request for money.

The elbows of the wealthy would have been raw with the touches of those who came begging for help, big help, for the mission to convert the Irish and we can be sure that enthusiasm for the cause was far from universal. There must have been the usual crowd who would have nothing to do with it and who let it be known that they considered the Irish – and Patrick – to be mad.

This was the first foreign mission in the history of the world. Up to this time the preaching of the Gospel had been confined to the Roman Empire and there were those who argued that it was unnatural to baptise the Irish because they were uncivilised. No one dared to say that the empire was going down the tubes and that any Christian, lay or cleric, could baptise whoever they liked wherever they liked. Mind you there were some, including Patrick himself, who were courageous enough to suggest that all baptised people might be numbered among the citizens of Rome. Was it not a Christian Empire? A debate began to rage and it might have continued not just for a year or two but for decades – as long as Patrick continued with his work in Ireland and continued to send back begging letters which, as everyone agreed, contained some very exciting stories.

You might think that, with the passing of the years, his critics would eventually be silenced but people who like to complain about other people's use of money are never silenced. Eventually something happened which made them dance for joy. Patrick's friend, in whom he had confided about that incident when he was fourteen, had kept that secret to himself for many years. He heard all the criticisms of Patrick and his mission and of his begging letters looking for vast sums of money and it wore him down. He decided that, after thirty years, he could no longer hold the secret to himself so, with great relief, he revealed Patrick's adolescent indiscretion to the world (CP, 32).

Eyes popped, ears twitched and jaws dropped. If a man like Patrick could behave like that when he was fourteen, what was likely to do as he got older? People became very concerned about all that money which had been sent to him over the years. People shuddered at the thought but, on the very night when he had heard that his friend had betrayed his confidence, Patrick had one of his dreams. We will talk about that later.

As we all know there is more to money than bags of gold. People love money. Money fertilises the imagination. If we know that someone has money we think about them, we wonder about them, we admire them; we smile at their every gesture and stand amazed at their every achievement, however trivial. All is well and all remains well until those people with money do something unbecoming of their exalted status and then a howl of righteous indignation will rise up. So it was with Patrick after his friend told everyone about that episode of his youth. Everyone had the same question on their lips: He did what?!

It was a public relations disaster but Patrick, being a man of initiative, sat down to write what the world now calls his *Confession*, 'I Patrick, a sinner and a bogman, least of all God's faithful and despised by many' (CP, 1).

CHAPTER 12

Coroticus!

Nobody likes slavery except the slave owner and those that profit from him. A slave might love a master but no slave will love slavery, though they might have to be careful about saying so, because they cannot ignore the day-to-day reality of being owned. If, on the other hand, a slave has managed to escape and to live a free life, part of that freedom is the ability to hate with a pure passion the evil that they have endured. Patrick was one of those and his New York friend would have admired him for it.

Patrick's greatest joy in Ireland was baptism. He baptised thousands of people and the sight of the newly baptised, in their fine white robes, always made him want to praise God. With every passing year his flock was growing in numbers and he loved them all. On this particular day of baptism Patrick might have had to leave the celebrations early and take to the road. Wherever he was, we are not sure how he got the news that the men, whom he had just baptised, had been killed and the women been taken off as slaves. We do know that he wrote a letter and we have some idea what was in it. It might have read like this:

> I, Patrick, in the name of Christ writing to Coroticus, a fellow citizen in the glorious and holy empire of Rome. I write of men slaughtered and women taken captive. Did you not see their white robes? Did you not ask why, in this heathen land, they were dressed in this manner? Did it not awaken any memory of that most holy day of baptism? You have shed innocent blood. The men are now with the saints in heaven but you have placed yourself in danger of hell fire until you deliver those Christian women, whom you hold captive, from defilement and hand them over to the care of the priest of God who carries this letter.

Patrick had preached the Gospel in Ireland for thirty years. He was a famous man both in Ireland itself and in Britannia and he knew that Coroticus had heard of him. He summoned a young Irish priest whom he himself had educated and told him to go after Coroticus and deliver the letter (LC, 3). We do not know how long it took him to do this but we do know that, when the young man finally returned, he came with bad news.

He had been instructed to tell Coroticus that he was speaking in Patrick's name but, when he had finished, Coroticus and his men said nothing. They just looked at him in silence and then they laughed at his accent. Some of the captive women recognised Patrick's young messenger and they called out to him, but Coroticus' soldiers beat them into silence. The young man was told to go and tell his mad bishop that those women would be sold to the Picts.

When Patrick heard this he sat down to write a second letter:

With my own hand I have written and composed these words, to be given delivered and sent to the soldiers of Coroticus. I do not say, to my fellow citizens, or to fellow citizens of the holy Romans, but to fellow citizens of the demons because of their evil works. (LC, 2)

He addressed this second letter to the 'holy and humble of heart', pleading with them not to flatter 'such people' or to take food or drink with them or even receive alms from them: 'Which of the saints would not be horrified to make merry and to enjoy a feast with such people?' (LC, 13).

This was a letter of excommunication, not just denouncing Coroticus but excluding him from the Church and Patrick wanted those who read it to be clear that he had every right to do this. He admitted to being a sinful and ignorant man, but he was a bishop and he was writing this letter in his own hand. He knew he had his critics: 'I live for my God to teach the pagans even if I am despised by some' (LC, 1).

The Irish had taken him captive and 'wreaked havoc on the slaves and hand maids of my father's house' but now he was a slave in Christ for 'that remote pagan people' (LC, 10). He warned his own people that, if they did not recognise him, they were not 'of the same sheepfold' nor did they have 'one God as Father' (LC, 11). Patrick insisted that God had put 'this eagerness into my heart' by which he meant his love for the Irish and especially for the victims of Coroticus: 'Wild wolves have swallowed up the flock of the Lord, which was indeed growing excellently in Ireland with the greatest loving care' (LC, 12).

He called out to those who had been killed – 'a crime so horrible and unspeakable'. He grieved for them and yet 'thanks be to God, as baptized faithful people, you have departed from this world to paradise' (LC, 17). They would reign with the apostles, the prophets and the martyrs. They would gain an everlasting kingdom.

There was no such joy for those 'who are banished and deported to distant lands where sin openly, gravely and shamelessly abounds' (LC, 15). He grieved for them, being reduced to slavery 'among the most degraded most vile apostates and Picts' (LC, 15). Those who distribute baptised women as prizes will 'perish from the face of the Lord' (LC, 19). Patrick wanted his letter to be read 'before all the people, even in the presence of Coroticus himself' (LC, 21) and his soldiers, so that God might inspire them to come to their senses and repent of their crimes and 'release the baptised captive women whom they had previously seized' (LC, 21).

Patrick's letter to Coroticus is not as well known as the story about Patrick and the snakes or the story of the shamrock. It is quite likely that the New York woman never heard of it but, if she did, she would have been proud of St Patrick, her friend, and she might even have joined him in his prayer that Coroticus and his soldiers would repent, 'that they may thus deserve to live for God and be made whole here and for eternity. Peace to the father and to the Son and to the Holy Spirit. Amen' (LC, 21).

CHAPTER 13

To the Ends of the Earth

Patrick was not particularly good at remembering his dreams. Sometimes all he could remember was a voice in the night as was the case with that first dream he had in Ireland: 'You have fasted well. Very soon you will return to your native country' (CP, 17). The second dream was much the same: 'Look – your ship is ready' (CP, 17). When he heard those words he knew what to do and he set out for home.

Often, when we have been through a tough time and the tough time comes to an end, that is the moment when we finally fall apart. This happened to Patrick after he escaped from slavery and made his way back to Gaul where he spent twenty-eight days wandering through a desolate landscape. It was not till after those pigs appeared and that blasphemous incident with the honey, that Patrick was tested by Satan. He tells us that he cried out and 'the splendour of the sun fell on me; and immediately, all that weight was lifted from me. I believe that I was helped by

Christ the Lord, and that his spirit cried out for me' (CP, 20).

His next dream, the big one, was about those letters from Ireland and the people by the wood of Voclut calling to him. He remembered what he saw in that dream – people near the wood of Vocult calling him back to Ireland. The whole world knows about this dream.

His next dream was peculiar as dreams often are. He saw someone but he did not know, 'God knows, whether it was within me or beside me' (CP, 24). He heard a voice speaking with authority, though he could not make out what was being said until the very end: 'The one who gave his life for you, he it is who speaks in you' (CP, 24).

Another time, he saw someone praying inside him. 'It was as if I were inside my body, and I heard him above me, that is, above my inner self, praying strongly, with sighs' (CP, 25). He was amazed and astonished, and wondered who was praying inside him but when he woke up he remembered the words of St Paul: 'The Spirit comes to help us in our weakness; for we do not know how to pray as we ought, but that very Spirit intercedes with sighs too deep for words' (Rom 8:26).

On the night after he heard that his teenage sin had been laid bare before the world, he had a dream in which he saw writing 'before my dishonored face' He heard a voice: 'He who touches you touches the apple of my eye' (CP, 29).

One more time, when he had been taken captive yet again by Irish heathens, he heard a divine voice: 'you will be with them for two months' (CP, 21). Sixty days later he was set free. As he grew older he could feel God's love drawing closer.

Patrick had no time for those who worshiped the sun that rises every day and sets every night. That sun will never reign nor will its splendor continue forever. He believed in 'the true sun, that is, Christ, who will never perish' (CP, 60). Towards the end of his Confession Patrick got a bit carried away. He even said that he wanted to shed his blood 'with these converts and captives' (CP, 59). That did not happen but, instead of bloodshed, he left us with written words:

> Again and again I briefly put before you the words of my Confession. I testify in truth and in great joy of heart before God and his holy angels that I never had any other reason for returning to that nation from which I had earlier escaped, except the gospel and God's promises. (CP, 61)

> I pray for those who believe in and have reverence for God. Some of them may happen to inspect or come upon this writing which Patrick, a sinner without learning, wrote in Ireland. May none of them ever say that whatever little I did or made known to please God was done through ignorance. Instead, you can judge and believe in all truth that it was a gift of God.

> This is my confession before I die. (CP, 62)

Patrick died. We are not quite sure how, but he was old enough to die and people had enough sense to care for the words which you have just read. They were kept safe. His story was told again and again. The people of Ireland turned to Christ. They loved Patrick as their saint and shortly afterwards Irish monks would travel across Europe like him, preaching the Gospel and founding monasteries. Many centuries later Irish people would travel to every part of the world with their story of a youth who had been a slave in their land, who escaped, and who later returned to the people who enslaved him.

Then one day I stood in Saint Patrick's Cathedral in New York looking at that woman praying to the patron saint of my land. She had a message for me: 'You Irish have a claim on him but you do not own him. He belongs to everybody who wants to stop hating, everybody who wants to love those who do them wrong'.

Helpful links:
The Confessions of Saint Patrick at www.confessio.ie
Letter to the soldiers of Coroticus at
www.confessio.ie/etexts/epistola_english#
The Martin Luther King, Jr. Center for Nonviolent
Social Change at www.thekingcenter.org

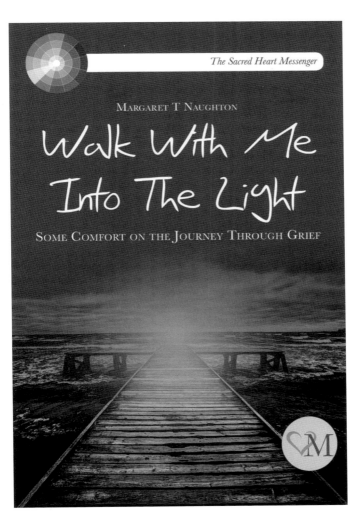

WWW.MESSENGER.IE
TEL: 01 7758522
€3.99

The Sacred Heart Messenger

BEING THERE

A COMPANION ON THE PATHWAY OF ILLNESS

MARGARET T NAUGHTON

Author of *Walk With Me Into The Light: Some Comfort on the Journey Through Grief*

WWW.MESSENGER.IE
TEL: 01 7758522
€3.99

WWW.MESSENGER.IE
TEL: 01 7758522
€3.99

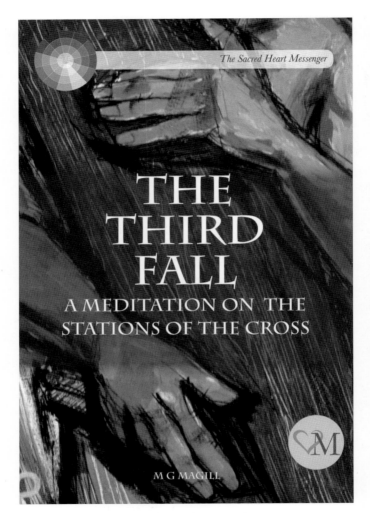

The Sacred Heart Messenger

THE THIRD FALL

A MEDITATION ON THE STATIONS OF THE CROSS

M G MAGILL

WWW.MESSENGER.IE
TEL: 01 7758522
€3.99